BELONGING

Reconnecting America's Loneliest Generation

Springtide™
RESEARCH INSTITUTE

A SPRINGTIDE™
A PROMISE.

TO YOU

. . . who are young, full of wonder and possibility. You who are navigating some of life's most important questions and most tumultuous waters. You who are sometimes flourishing and sometimes floundering and oftentimes both. You who are at once being and becoming.

We dedicate our work to your thriving.

We dedicate ourselves to understanding your inner and outer lives.

TO YOU

. . . who are fiercely devoted to young people. You who advocate for and walk alongside young people with steadiness. You who are unwavering amid the waves.

We offer our research as an aid to the role you already play.

We offer ourselves as allies in accompaniment.

TRIBUTE.
A PLEDGE.

 AND TO

. . . the waves that crash, the currents that bend and beckon, the dark depths, and the effervescent crests. To this all-important period of life: worthy of considered listening and faithful retelling, worthy of companionship, worthy of care.

We situate our work at this intersection of human and religious experience in the lives of young people: a space of ebb and flow, of calm and chaos, of clear and murky moments.

A space we are dedicated to exploring and engaging

 **WITH YOU.**

Springtide™
RESEARCH INSTITUTE

————

OUR MISSION

Compelled by the urgent desire to listen and attend to the lives of young people (ages 13 to 25), Springtide™ Research Institute is committed to understanding the distinct ways new generations experience and express community, identity, and meaning.

We exist at the intersection of religious and human experience in the lives of young people. And we're here to listen.

We combine quantitative and qualitative research to reflect and amplify the lived realities of young people as they navigate shifting social, cultural, and religious landscapes. By delivering fresh data and actionable insights, we equip those who care about young people to care better.

CONTENTS

Belonging is . . .

"[a] place that's open and where you can be known even in the complicated times . . . a place where all of that can be on the table and yet you're loved."

—Ophelia, 20

FOREWORD

Belonging: Reconnecting America's Loneliest Generation examines the intersection of two critical social currents in the lives of young people: declining trust in social institutions (religious and cultural) and rising social isolation resulting in severe loneliness. In short, we want to understand how and where young people can and do find belongingness amid these currents.

Belongingness: *The state or feeling of connectedness that arises when seen, known, and accepted by another.*

We express our gratitude to you and other like-hearted individuals and organizations, religious and cultural leaders, in making this study's findings known. In doing so, we join the important efforts to address the loneliness epidemic affecting America's youngest generation. We want to work with you in finding effective ways to reconnect young people to the institutions, the organizations, and most importantly, the adults who care about them across the domains of their lives—physically, mentally, emotionally, and spiritually.

INTRODUCTION

This report was born of our concern for the lives of young people. We are attuned to the dramatic rise of social isolation and loneliness among young people in America, as well as globally, reaching epidemic levels. We are also attuned to the dramatic decline of young people's trust in and affiliation with cultural and religious institutions. While faith communities and youth-serving organizations once served as trusted places of belonging and meaningful connection for young people, that is less and less the norm. Multiple studies, including this one, confirm the alarming and increasingly common experience of loneliness among young people but also their deep desire for meaningful connection to others.

A study conducted by the global health service company Cigna (2018) that surveyed more than 20,000 U.S. adults 18 years of age and older measured the impact of loneliness in America. Among their chief findings are two that most caught our attention:

- **Generation Z (adults ages 18 to 22) is the loneliest generation** and claims to be in worse health than older generations.

- **Social media use alone is not a predictor of loneliness;** respondents defined as very heavy users of social media have a loneliness score (43.5) that is not markedly different from the score of those who never use social media (41.7).

As we were analyzing the data from our study, Ford Motor Company released their 2020 Trends report. Their Chief Futurist identified loneliness as one of the most pressing issues confronting society now and for the foreseeable future. They note, "Trust in institutions and brands is declining, and our examination of loneliness suggests many people feel they lack trusting relationships with peers, too. Without the bedrock of trust, people feel increased anxiety."

Our study builds on the existing body of research by looking exclusively at America's youngest generations—young people ages 13 to 25. We wanted to know more about the causes of this alarming loneliness epidemic and its effects on young people's lives. We wanted to better understand where young people experience or do not experience belonging. We wanted to explore the relationship between the increasing experience of loneliness and the decreasing experience of belonging among young people. We had no idea what we would discover.

We found the data disturbing. The young people we surveyed had high rates of loneliness, social isolation, and stress. Many indicated they had few social interactions and few people they could turn to in times of trouble or even just to talk. So we were curious to learn what reduces loneliness and isolation and helps young people experience belongingness.

Frankly, we were stunned. Throughout the interview process, we kept asking questions about **where** young people felt a sense of belonging. We felt confident we would be able to produce a report that identified the hallmarks and characteristics of organizations that were getting it "right."

But every time we pushed young people to tell us **where**, they pushed back. Over and over, they would tell us **who**—who created a sense of belonging for them. It turns out, the place or setting didn't matter nearly as much as the relationships these young people had with family, friends, and caring adults.

This study has led us to a simple and powerful observation: connecting young people to more trusted adults in what we call "belonging relationships" is one antidote to their rampant loneliness and social isolation. **In other words, YOU are the antidote!**

Belonging relationship: A relationship that cultivates the state or feeling of belongingness in another.

Concrete actions can be taken to stem the rising tide of the loneliness and social isolation of young people by connecting them to the belonging relationships they desire. The actions required may surprise you. They may seem simple on the surface, but they will require an investment of time and intentionality in building a specific quality of relationship—a belonging relationship.

The findings in this report are based on the data of two recent Springtide™ Research initiatives. The first initiative was a survey conducted in the fall of 2019 using a nationally representative sample of 1,000 young people ages 13 to 25. This provided us with the quantitative data used for the report. The second initiative was 35 in-depth interviews with young people, conducted either in person or by phone in the fall of 2019. More detailed information on our methodology can be found in the appendix.

As you read and work, please drop us a line @WeAreSpringtide **on Facebook, Instagram, or Twitter, or at** *stories@springtideresearch.org*, **to let us know how cultivating belonging relationships is impacting the lives of the young people in your circle of care.**

SECTION I:
THE LANDSCAPE OF LONELINESS

FIRST FINDING
MANY YOUNG PEOPLE ARE LONELY

Our national survey was directed at identifying the extent of young people's experience of loneliness, social isolation, and stress. For our purposes, we define *loneliness* as "a persistent state of being in which a person feels isolated, unsupported, and without close friends." Social isolation is closely related, as it is the state of having no or little contact with societal organizations or groups. Loneliness and social isolation are almost always connected in an individual's experience.

Loneliness: A persistent state of being in which a person feels isolated, unsupported, and without close friends.

To understand the impact of loneliness and social isolation, we employed UCLA's Loneliness Index, a widely used set of twenty questions that identify the experience of loneliness and social isolation from different perspectives. To each statement, respondents answered "never," "rarely," "sometimes," "always." The chart on page 16 shows the percentage of respondents, ages 13 to 25, who answered "sometimes" or "always" to each question.

Young People's Experience of Loneliness

Percentages of 13-to-25-year-olds who AGREE (responding "sometimes" or "always") with each statement.

● **Total Sample**
● **Those Who Attend Religious Gatherings**

I have nobody to talk to.

39%
36%

I feel completely alone.

33%
30%

I feel as if no one understands me.

45%
43%

No one really knows me well.

36%
33%

It is difficult for me to make friends.

41%
38%

 SPRINGTIDE™ NATIONAL RESEARCH RESULTS
© 2020 Springtide. Cite, share, and join the conversation at *springtideresearch.org*.

These responses are troubling. They indicate that one in three of our young people feel completely alone much of the time. Forty-five percent feel as if no one understands them. Nearly 40% have no one to talk to and feel left out. The statistics are devastating; the human consequences are heartbreaking.

Religious institutions have historically been sources of connection, so we were curious if these same percentages held for young people who attended some type of religious gathering.

One in three
of our young people feel completely alone much of the time.

Nearly 40%
have no one to talk to and feel left out.

As you see, when compared to the overall sample (see page 16) there is very little difference between the total population and those youth who participate in religious groups. **Participating in religious groups has virtually no protective effect against the experience of loneliness.** Over 37% of young people who attend religious groups still say that they have no one they can talk to. Over one in ten (12%) of young people who attend religious gatherings feel left out *all* the time. Where we expected to find a buffer between a young person and the rising tide of isolation, we found only more loneliness.

> 66 Where we expected to find a buffer between a young person and the rising tide of isolation, we found only more loneliness. 99

Clearly, merely participating in a religious community's activities does not lead to a fuller sense of belonging and diminished feelings of loneliness. And this experience is not only found in young people attending religious groups. Our data shows that this experience of widespread loneliness extends to young people participating in other organizations (sports teams, school clubs, service clubs, country clubs, professional associations, and other groups).

SECOND FINDING

MANY YOUNG PEOPLE ARE SOCIALLY ISOLATED

Next, we turn our attention to the experience of social isolation. Social isolation is the experience of feeling like an outsider, without any meaningful connection to a social group. The experiences of loneliness and social isolation commonly go together but are not necessarily connected. That is, a person may not experience loneliness but can still feel like an outsider, like they do not belong. To assess young people's experience of social isolation, we again used our survey responses to specific questions from UCLA's Loneliness Index. We discovered that the experience of social isolation closely parallels the experience of loneliness, with similar high percentages reporting feelings of social isolation.

Social isolation: The state of having no or little contact or experience of belonging to societal organizations or groups.

Young People's Experience of Social Isolation

Percentages of 13-to-25-year-olds who AGREE (responding "always" or "sometimes") with each statement.

 **Always**    **Sometimes**   Total

I have nobody to talk to.

- 8%
- 31%
- 39%

I feel left out.

- 12%
- 27%
- 39%

My social relationships are superficial.

- 7%
- 24%
- 31%

People are around me but not with me.

- 10%
- 28%
- 38%

I feel isolated from others.

- 10%
- 25%
- 35%

 SPRINGTIDE™ NATIONAL RESEARCH RESULTS
© 2020 Springtide. Cite, share, and join the conversation at *springtideresearch.org*.

Again, these statistics are alarming. **Ten percent of young people ALWAYS feel isolated from others. Twelve percent ALWAYS feel left out.** Our interviews illuminate this experience of social isolation. Here's how two of the young people interviewed describe it:

> **"It kind of felt like I was tagging along and like looking through binoculars [at] a group of people. . . . There's a very weird sense, like lesser. . . . I was very, very ostracized. . . . From my outside perspective, it seemed like everyone got along so well and everyone knew each other so well that I was reluctant to get in on it. . . . They all got really close, really fast, and I did not. And so I didn't feel like I belonged." (Chris, 19)**

> **"People would circle up and start talking together and I would be on the outside and wouldn't feel like . . . I could try to get into this, [and] they're probably not going to engage with me." (Alex, 22)**

DAILY MEANINGFUL SOCIAL INTERACTIONS

We also asked about this issue of social isolation in another way, by asking the young people how many meaningful interactions they had with other people on a typical day. Their responses are summarized in this pie chart.

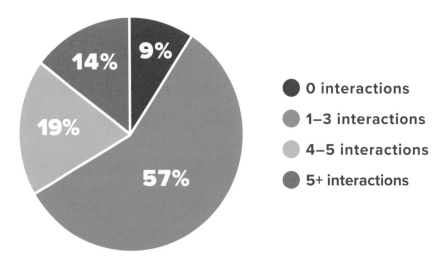

SPRINGTIDE™ NATIONAL RESEARCH RESULTS
© 2020 Springtide. Cite, share, and join the conversation at *springtideresearch.org*.

Nearly 10% had no meaningful social interactions in a typical day! Two-thirds (66%) of young people report having 3 or fewer meaningful interactions on a typical day. With these high percentages of young people lacking meaningful social interactions, it is not surprising that nearly 40% feel as if no one knows them.

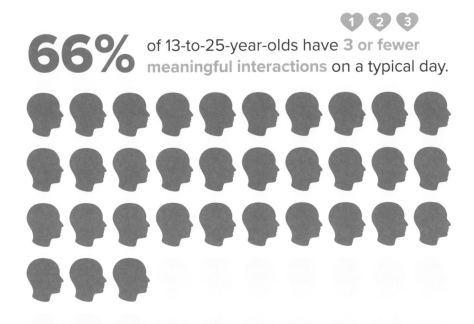

66% of 13-to-25-year-olds have **3 or fewer meaningful interactions** on a typical day.

SPRINGTIDE™ **NATIONAL RESEARCH RESULTS**
© 2020 Springtide. Cite, share, and join the conversation at *springtideresearch.org*.

" Nearly 40% of young people feel
at times as if no one knows them. "

A determining factor in young people's feeling of belongingness is the experience of being known by others.

———

"You'll have a deeper sense of belonging because people will know who you are. . . . It's not just knowing people in the group but the people knowing you. . . . It's not enough to just be like, 'I'm a part of this group.' It needs to be like, 'We're so glad Chris is here,' like because they know who I am."

(Chris, 19)

THIRD FINDING

MANY YOUNG PEOPLE ARE STRESSED

Closely connected to loneliness and social isolation are the feelings many young people experience of serious mental, emotional, and spiritual distress. For example, over half of the young people we surveyed reported having a difficult time feeling relaxed. Not surprisingly, stress and anxiety make it more difficult to connect with others, amplifying the effects of being lonely. Becca (14) told us, "I'm a generally anxious person so I don't like talking to people I don't know, but talking to people I do know—even if not well—is a lot easier than talking to complete strangers."

To explore the experience of stress in young people's lives, we included several stress-related questions in the survey. The young people's responses indicated high levels of stress across several factors.

YOUNG PEOPLE AND STRESS

Over 50% of 13-to-25-year-olds experience multiple stress factors.

58%

I feel stressed and overwhelmed overall.

66%

I feel like I don't have enough time to get everything done.

60%

I feel fatigued or tired even when I wake after an adequate sleep.

56%

I have a hard time feeling relaxed.

SPRINGTIDE™ NATIONAL RESEARCH RESULTS

I have anxiety. I've had it [from] a young age, and that has caused me to not really trust people or to feel like—even though logically I know they invited me out—that they like me, they want to spend time with me. Then my mind tells me that they don't really want to spend time with me and they're just trying to be nice. I'm usually not the one who [likes to] initiate conversations with others or to invite somebody out because **I always feel uncomfortable.**

(Lauren, 24)

————

STRESS AND LONELINESS

Among the young people we surveyed, there is a widespread experience of feeling overwhelmed, stressed, and anxious. We wondered about the connection between stress and loneliness, and in the interviews, young people connected those dots. Notice how Lauren (see page 31) connects anxiety with her inability to trust other people and to feel liked by them. Her anxiety also prevents her from reaching out to others.

Again, we were curious about the impact of participating in secular or religious groups on the experience of stress in young people. When we examined this connection, we saw little reduction in the young people's experiences of stress and anxiety. Merely participating in these organizations did not lead to less stress.

However, conversely, we found in the interviews with young people that **a gesture as simple as being acknowledged** in one of these settings could positively affect one's sense of stress.

> **"I'm not very religious, [but] this chapel seems very welcoming. I think like just having people sit next to me and seeing my professors and having them wave to me from across [the room] or like saying hi when they were walking up and down the aisle, that felt like I was actually being seen." (Carlie, 21)**

The clear implication of this data is that if we want to address the issues of loneliness and social isolation and increase young people's sense of belongingness, we also need to help young people with their feelings of stress and anxiety.

35%

Thirty-five percent of young people ages 13 to 25 say that they have no one to turn to when they're stressed.

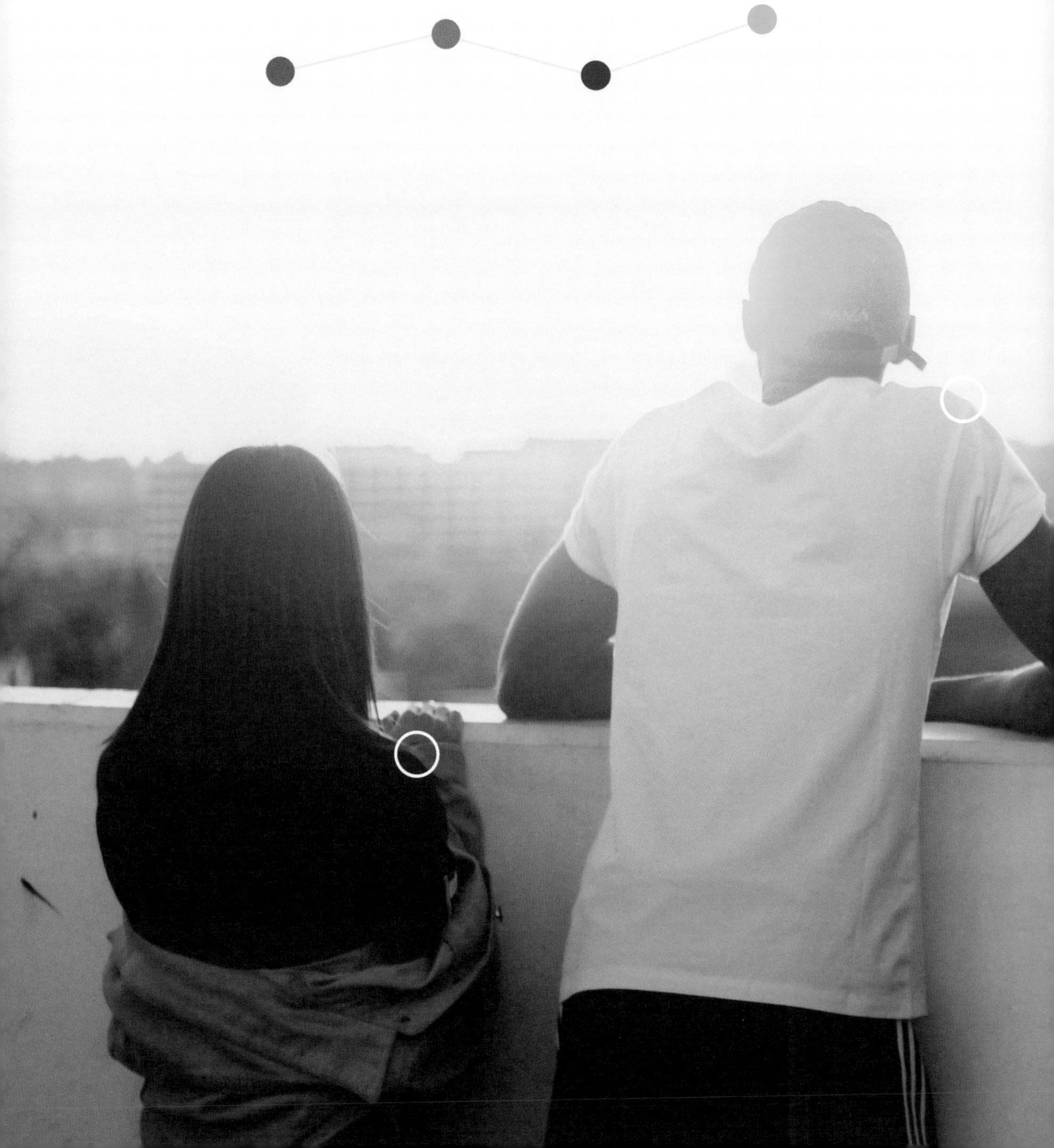

SECTION 2:
CREATING BELONGINGNESS

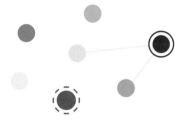

FOURTH FINDING

PARTICIPATION IS NOT BELONGING

Membership, just joining or just participating, is not enough to decrease loneliness, social isolation, or stress. This finding might seem surprising, especially to people from older generations. Many people from older generations could tell stories of how belonging to civic and religious institutions was—and perhaps still is—the way they made lifelong friends and found support and purpose for their life's work. Our research finds this is no longer the reality for many, if not most, young people. They have less trust in institutions than prior generations and as a result are moving away from them as places of belonging.

In the interviews we conducted, a number of the young people told us this very clearly. For example, Mark (24) told us: "Groups, organizations, and institutions have no effect on me as a person. I am who I am through experiences and those around me." Erick (25) said, "I started thinking through it and realized I don't want to be a part of that [religious] institution."

Other recent studies have found that institutional trust is at an all-time low, and it's been trending downward across nearly every meaningful social institution for nearly 50 years. This points to a shifting social landscape rather than a specific deficiency of any particular institution. While the decline of religious affiliation, especially among the younger generations, has garnered much public attention in recent years, people aren't just losing confidence in organized religion. They are losing trust in *all* social institutions.

> **People aren't just losing confidence in organized religion. They are losing trust in *all* social institutions.**

When we asked young people how institutions inform their sense of belonging, many stated that belonging is not about an institution at all, but rather the relationships they have and an internal "feeling" of being significant to others. Isaiah (19) put it this way: "I believe I most belong as an individual [in] my immediate community of friends and family."

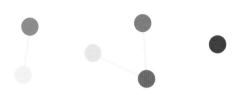

Gallup Poll on People's Confidence in Institutions

These numbers represent Gallup's percentages of the US population, 18 years and older, who had "a great deal" or "quite a lot" of confidence in these institutions. Note the precipitous drop in confidence from the 1970s to 2019.

Institution	1970s	2019
Big Business	26%	23%
The Medical System	80%	36%
The Presidency	52%	38%
Television News	46%	18%
Congress	42%	11%
Newspapers	39%	23%
Public Schools	58%	29%
Banks	60%	30%
Organized Religion	65%	36%

YOUNG PEOPLE'S Trust in Institutions

On a scale of 1 to 10, over 60% of 13-to-25-year-olds in our study rank their trust level at 5 or lower for all institutions except nonprofits.

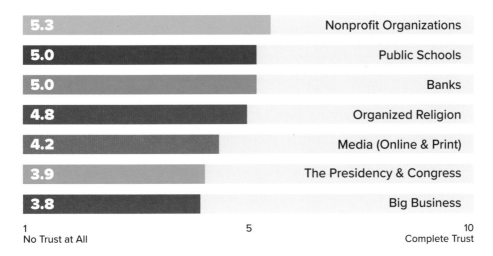

5.3	Nonprofit Organizations
5.0	Public Schools
5.0	Banks
4.8	Organized Religion
4.2	Media (Online & Print)
3.9	The Presidency & Congress
3.8	Big Business

1
No Trust at All

5

10
Complete Trust

SPRINGTIDE™ NATIONAL RESEARCH RESULTS
© 2020 Springtide. Cite, share, and join the conversation at *springtideresearch.org*.

Young people's low levels of trust in institutions sheds light on our earlier finding, that participation in secular and religious groups does not lead to decreased feelings of loneliness, social isolation, or stress. When young people have little confidence in an institution, they have little incentive to look for belonging in that institution. And many young people who do participate in these institutions fail to find belongingness within them (see Second Finding on page 21).

Let's take religious groups as one example. Churches, synagogues, temples, and other religious communities once were places we looked to for belongingness, but increasingly young people are not looking to our places of worship. **Nearly 25% of young people who attend worship gatherings weekly or more still feel as though no one understands them.** In fact, one-third of young people who report feeling completely alone also say they have become *more* religious in the last year. An increase in religious identification is not associated with a rise in belongingness.

66 An increase in religious identification is not associated with a rise in belongingness. 99

However, there is more to the story.

We discovered that young people who have a relationship with at least one trusted adult in a religious institution are more trusting, less isolated, less stressed, and more confident about their future. In other words, attending religious services does not reduce loneliness, but a relationship with even one trusted adult in a religious organization does.

> " Young people who have a relationship with a trusted adult in a religious institution are more trusting, less isolated, less stressed, more confident about their future, and more connected. "

In our interviews, the young people made it clear that when they encounter a group in which they find belongingness, it's because of the people and the relationships they experience. In other words, belongingness is generated by relationships not programs. The next finding makes it clear that the quality or nature of those relationships can profoundly affect one's experience of isolation or belongingness.

Impact of Trusted Adults for Young People Attending Religious Groups

Percentages of 13-to-25-year-olds who AGREE with each statement.

● **0 Trusted Adults**   ● 1+ Trusted Adults

I feel completely alone.

32%

14%

I feel stressed overall.

58%

44%

● **0 Trusted Adults**   ● 1+ Trusted Adults

I am confident about where I am at in life.

61%

73%

S **SPRINGTIDE™ NATIONAL RESEARCH RESULTS**
© 2020 Springtide. Cite, share, and join the conversation at *springtideresearch.org*.

FIFTH FINDING

THE IMPACT OF TRUSTED ADULTS

As part of this research, we were curious about the role trusted adults play in young people's lives, especially in relation to young people's experiences of belonging or lack of belonging. A trusted adult is someone a young person can turn to if they are in trouble or need someone to talk to.

What we discovered is more encouraging than we expected. Yes, family, peer groups, and social gatherings are important sources of connection and belonging for young people, but relationships with trusted adults appear to be just as important, if not more important. That is, of course, if the relationships meet certain conditions.

Trusted adult: *An adult a young person can turn to if they are in trouble or need someone to talk to.*

In the survey and interviews, young people consistently affirmed the importance of having supportive relationships with family and peers. The survey data also clearly shows a strong connection between having relationships with other trusted adults and diminished feelings of loneliness, isolation, and stress.

Trusted Adults and Decreased Feelings of Loneliness, Social Isolation, and Stress

Percentages of 13-to-25-year-olds who AGREE with each statement.

● **I feel completely alone.**
Youth with more trusted adults
in their lives have decreased
feelings of loneliness.

● **No one understands me.**
Youth with more trusted adults
in their lives have decreased
feelings of not being understood.

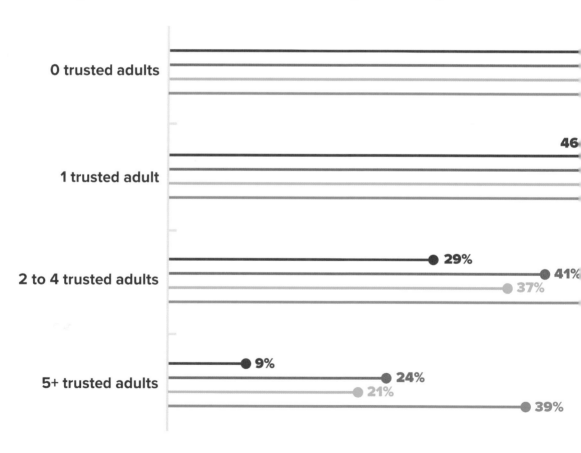

0 trusted adults

1 trusted adult   46

2 to 4 trusted adults   29%   41%   37%

5+ trusted adults   9%   24%   21%   39%

SPRINGTIDE™ NATIONAL RESEARCH RESULTS
© 2020 Springtide. Cite, share, and join the conversation at *springtideresearch.org*.

I feel left out.

Youth with more trusted adults in their lives have decreased feelings of being left out.

● **62%**
● **70%**
● **59%**
● **73%**

● **60%**
● **52%**
● **68%**

● **57%**

I feel stressed and overwhelmed.

Youth with more trusted adults in their lives have decreased feelings of being stressed.

As this data shows, when young people have trusted adults in their lives there is a connection with decreased feelings of loneliness, isolation, and stress. A relationship with even one trusted adult results in a 16% decrease in feelings of loneliness. Going from no trusted adults to having 2 to 4 trusted adults leads to a 29% decrease in not feeling understood and a 22% decrease in feeling left out. Unfortunately, nearly 1 in 10 young people do not have a trusted adult at all, and 23% have only one trusted adult.

Trusted adults also reduce the experience of social isolation.

- Just one trusted adult in the life of a young person cuts severe isolation in half.

- Young people are four times more likely to feel understood overall if they have even just one trusted adult in their life.

- Nearly 20% of young people with one trusted adult in their life ALWAYS feel as though they are understood.

The data confirms just how important trusted adults are in the lives of young people. While this may have always been the case, the shifting of social life away from regular meaningful interaction with trusted adults makes it an even more urgent task. The new social reality demands a renewed dedication to building relationships between young people and trusted adults. It may feel like you are doing nothing when you sit and listen, honestly and without judgment, to a young person. You're not doing nothing. You are doing the very thing necessary to reduce their experience of social isolation, loneliness, and stress.

Number of Trusted Adults in Young People's Lives

Percentages of trusted adults in a 13-to-25-year-old's life.

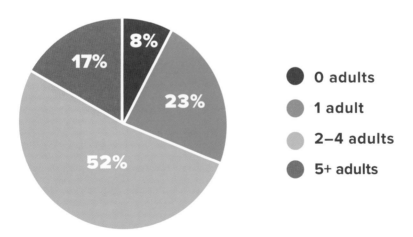

- 0 adults
- 1 adult
- 2–4 adults
- 5+ adults

SPRINGTIDE™ NATIONAL RESEARCH RESULTS
© 2020 Springtide. Cite, share, and join the conversation at *springtideresearch.org*.

Ellie

Ellie (22) arrived at Wheaton College in Illinois without a ready-made community to settle into. She discovered that some of the student-led communities she tried lacked a level of accountability that she values.

"I have not been able to be as involved in student-led communities like I had anticipated. I noticed that there was not always a consistent welcoming authority in the environment overseeing the student's endeavors. Even if there was a solid group, students would not always show up or follow through with responsibilities. Communities that I thought I would enjoy—such as floor nights, student clubs, dances, floor dinners—did not maintain a level of commitment or consistency from the participants."

Ellie eventually found a feeling of belonging within a CrossFit program and a Bible study group. Both were led by caring adults that Ellie formed a relationship with.

"The way CrossFit's community is unique is that there is usually the same coach working with a certain class every time. The coach gets to know you, is supportive of your goals and what you want to accomplish. It's like a mentorship, with the coach as fitness and life mentor," she said. "If you've had a bad day, the coach will ask, 'How's it going? What's going on? Have you had a rough week?' and if I was sad or upset, I felt comfortable to walk into this place, share my concerns, work hard at something that relieved my stress, and empathize with others who are most likely going through the same thing."

Ellie finds that same level of holistic care shown by her Bible study hostess, she said. "The hostess makes dinner, wants to get to know us, cares about us. Anytime you need a meal, she says, 'Let's sit down.' If there is something going on, she says, 'Let me help you.' She helped me pick up my first car, and allowed me to store things in her basement over the summer. She shows me that she is someone who is willing to express her love. Nothing seems to be too much of a burden for her. She's not just having the Bible study over for Sunday night, but she invites us into her house as capable adults who need some motherly care for a few hours. If I miss a meeting, she always says, 'We missed you last week. How you doing? You all right?' and is able to empathize in a way that is nonjudgmental, like she is willing to give of herself if need be."

**Belonging relationships
have certain qualities:**

welcome, warmth, supportiveness,

authenticity, vulnerability, honesty, curiosity,

invitation, openness, accountability

SECTION 3:
TURNING THE TIDE

ACTIONABLE INSIGHTS FOR CULTIVATING BELONGINGNESS

Springtide undertakes research to deliver fresh data that yields actionable insights in order to equip those who care about young people to care better. To that end, we present two insights and immediate actions that can significantly reduce the alarming levels of social isolation, loneliness, and stress in young people's lives.

In essence, we see in the data that **increasing the number of trusted adults in a young person's life is a critical response to severe loneliness, social isolation, and stress. The more trusted adults in a young person's life, the greater the experience of belongingness for that young person.**

Insight One

As the number of trusted adults in a young person's life increases, their reported feelings of loneliness, social isolation, and stress decrease. And not just slightly: by a strikingly significant degree!

Percentages of 13-to-25-year-olds who AGREE with each statement.

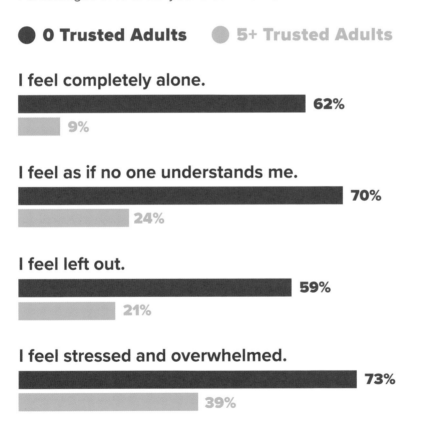

● **0 Trusted Adults**   ● **5+ Trusted Adults**

I feel completely alone.
- 62%
- 9%

I feel as if no one understands me.
- 70%
- 24%

I feel left out.
- 59%
- 21%

I feel stressed and overwhelmed.
- 73%
- 39%

SPRINGTIDE™ NATIONAL RESEARCH RESULTS
© 2020 Springtide. Cite, share, and join the conversation at *springtideresearch.org*.

When we look at the data on page 58, we see this vividly. About 62% of young people who have no trusted adult relationships report feeling completely alone. That number drops to only 9% for young people who have five or more trusted adult relationships. That's an astonishing 86% reduction in young people feeling completely alone.

> 66 Severe loneliness, social isolation, and stress can be substantially reduced by increasing the number of connections young people have to trusted adults. 99

We see this same pattern on young people's reported experience of feeling as if "no one understands me." Around 70% of those with no trusted adult relationships report feeling this way, while that figure drops to 24% for those with five or more trusted adult relationships. The same is true for "feeling left out": 59% of those with no trusted adult relationships report this experience, but that number drops substantially to 21% for those with five or more trusted adult relationships. While the stress factor "I feel stressed and overwhelmed" had the lowest reported discrepancy between those with and without trusted adult relationships (73% for those with no trusted adult relationships, dropping to 39% for those with five or more trusted adult relationships), it is still a significant margin.

The data is clear: severe loneliness, social isolation, and stress can be substantially reduced by increasing the number of connections young people have to trusted adults.

ACTION: Increase the number of trusted adult relationships in young people's lives.

Connecting young people to even just one additional trusted adult can reduce their feelings of loneliness, isolation, and stress. But the benefits of connecting young people to five or more trusted adults is a game-changing prospect and ought to be our goal.

How can we achieve the biggest impact? A study by Cacioppo et al., "Alone in the Crowd: The Structure and Spread of Loneliness in a Large Social Network" (2009), offers this perspective:

> **"The results advance our understanding of the broad social forces that drive loneliness and suggest that efforts to reduce loneliness in our society may benefit by aggressively targeting the people in the periphery to help repair their social networks and to create a protective barrier against loneliness that can keep the whole network from unraveling."**

In other words, the biggest impact can be made by focusing our efforts on the 31% of young people who have one or no trusted adult relationships currently. And doing so is the most urgent task before us. Who are the young people on the margins of your community, society, institution, or club? Who is floating between groups, on the periphery of various communities, not fully connected to any group or trusted adult? How can you reach those young people?

Insight Two

Young people's experiences of belongingness can be cultivated by trusted adults, and belongingness deepens through an identifiable process. We call this the Belongingness Process.

We know that young people initially enter relationships, groups, clubs, and organizations because of certain commonalities—shared interests, values, beliefs, practices, vocations, or professions. But they stay in those relationships when they feel like they belong.

In analyzing the interview data, we observed a clear pattern in the stories of young people as they moved from joining a group to ultimately experiencing true belonging within that group. Over and over again, three distinct experiences showed up in their narratives: feeling noticed, feeling named, and feeling known. These experiences build on one another to deepen the overall experience of belonging. This movement sometimes happens quickly and sometimes more slowly.

The word *feeling* in each of these instances isn't a reference to a fleeting emotional state or episode. It is a reference to a felt reality: a true, lasting, and concrete experience that invites and allows a relationship to flourish and deepen.

> 66 Over and over again, three distinct experiences showed up in their narratives: feeling noticed, feeling named, and feeling known. 99

THE BELONGINGNESS PROCESS

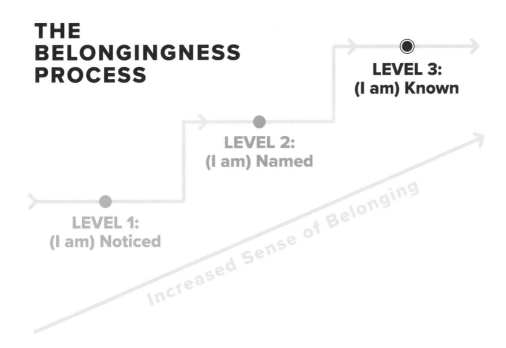

LEVEL 3:
(I am) Known

LEVEL 2:
(I am) Named

LEVEL 1:
(I am) Noticed

Increased Sense of Belonging

LEVEL 1: (I am) Noticed

The perception of "being noticed" by another—being seen or acknowledged, even in the most straightforward ways—is the initial step toward a sense of belonging. It is here that young people describe the power of being invited into the relationship and having others become interested in them. The simple act of *seeing* generates an initial sense of belongingness for a young person, which creates a foundation for deeper relationships. For Carlie (21), having her professors "wave to me from across the [room]" and "say hi" when they passed in the hall was enough to generate her initial sense of belongingness on campus.

> 66 The simple act of *seeing* generates an initial sense of belongingness for a young person, which creates a foundation for deeper relationships. 99

The experience of feeling seen is incredibly powerful. Hannah (21) describes a relationship in which her sense of belonging began with being seen, noting, "She saw me. She's the one that would invite me to dinner. . . . She just makes me feel like I belong. She'll take me with her. She pulled me out of my comfort zone, and she gave me that sense of confidence."

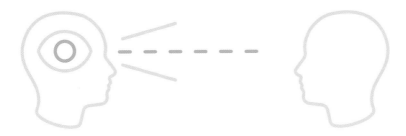

ACTION: Give a young person the experience of being noticed.

A helpful reflection to more effectively establish this level of belongingness for a young person is to first pay attention to how you are paying attention. What are you hearing the other say? What are you observing in their body language? What do you notice about how they are feeling? In order to pay attention, you must be fully present. Can you imagine how rare the experience is for a young person to have a trusted adult who is fully present to them, making them feel as if nothing matters more in this moment than paying attention to their life? This is the action needed at this level of belonging.

LEVEL 2: (I am) Named

Rabbi Jonathan Sacks defines community as "that place where I am known by name and missed if I were gone." To be named by another is significant both in literal and metaphorical ways. It is a way to communicate the felt experience of being known, which is a vulnerable and important experience that paves the way to an abiding sense of belongingness. It builds on and deepens the sense that one is *noticed*.

On a metaphorical level, being named also refers to the initial stages of becoming known by another or others. As young people open themselves up to others, knowing and being known deepens their relationships. Said Chris (19), "You'll have a deeper sense of belonging because people will know who you are. [It's] not just knowing people in the group but the people knowing you. They know who I am."

> **"** Calling, welcoming, and greeting a young person by name is an instant way to forge a connection. **"**

So knowing a person starts with knowing their name. Think of all that a name conveys: it is inextricably connected to a person's identity. Calling, welcoming, and greeting a young person by name is an instant way to forge a connection. The simple use of a person's name triggers an immediate connection. It demonstrates that the young person in your life is known in one of the most basic yet powerful ways.

ACTION: Commit to knowing the names of the young people in your community.

When you learn a young person's name, confirm that you are using their expressed pronouns and proper pronunciation. Memorize their name and use it three times in conversation soon after learning it, and again in every passing or gathering. Deepen the felt experience of being named by becoming curious about the young person's life. Ask questions that result in them feeling like they are beginning to be known by you on a deeper level. These questions will help you to begin to know a young person's fears, anxieties, hopes, and joys.

LEVEL 3: (I am) Known

While becoming known is a process, it deepens and reaches another level of belongingness when a person begins feeling truly safe in a relationship or community. This depth of belongingness builds on the first two levels, being noticed and being named, but adds the all-important dimension of unreserved acceptance. Freed from the fear of rejection, young people feel safe having open, honest conversations about their lives—hopes, anxieties, challenges, and joys alike.

This kind of acceptance has immeasurable significance as an antidote for severe loneliness, isolation, and stress. We see clearly in the data that accepting young people without judgment is an essential condition for deep belongingness to occur. If a judgmental posture is present, belongingness is not possible. Gillian (22) described feeling judged as, "I feel very much like I do not belong in that space and that I can't sort of be myself in that space."

> 66 Accepting young people without judgment is an essential condition for deep belongingness to occur. 99

The profound importance of nonjudgment is described by young people in various ways, such as this description of a trusted adult:

> **She's interested in everybody's life . . . and so like [she] talks about the exciting things in [her] life and then [she's] also excited to talk about things in our lives. I've felt like I can share my heart with her and she might be sad for me, but she's going to encourage me, and it may be something that she could totally disapprove of, but she's never going to say like, "Why? Why are you doing this? You can't do this." . . . She's not judgmental that way." (Alex, 22)**

ACTION: Practice nonjudgment.

If you feel inclined to pass judgment when listening to stories, opinions, or ideas of a young person, try to ask questions to learn more about where they're coming from, and enter their worldview. Even if you disagree with their conclusions or decisions, make it clear that any disagreement is not a rejection of their personhood or their standing in your relationship or community.

ACTION: Be intentional.

Finally, when considering this noticed, named, known framework make sure you are intentional in its practice. As the old saying goes, **we measure what we value** and **we value what we measure.** Keep track of each young person with whom you come into contact using whatever way works best for you. For example, you might track the following:

- Have you noticed them? shown interest in them?

- Do you know their name? their interests, sorrows, and joys?

- Do they feel safe enough to talk about what really matters to them? Are they on the pathway to being known?

- Most importantly: Are you spending your time with the 31% of young people who have one or fewer trusted adults in their life? And have you been able to connect them to at least one additional trusted adult?

Moving young people from a state of loneliness and isolation is not something that happens by accident. It needs to be planned and intentional to effectively create a sense of belongingness.

Concluding Thoughts

One of the fundamental truths about communities that sociologists have long known is that *belonging* comes before *believing*. The data in this report confirms this reality. However, we often get that equation backward, especially when it comes to young people. We think that we must get everyone convicted of the same set of principles first, and then the community will emerge. This approach is not only ineffective but often leads young people to distrust organizations and disengage from them.

Durable, sustainable communities have always been built on a solid foundation of belonging. Using the insights in this report to create belongingness with young people will build a community of people with shared values, common concerns, and a great commitment to each other. It is critical that people feel like they are a part of the group, not just for their own psychological, spiritual, and physical health, but for the health of the groups, organizations, and institutions that make up our society. Understanding this truth has never been more important. None of us can come together while so many feel left out.

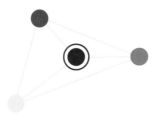

"A sense of belonging is a human need, just like the need for food and shelter. Feeling that you belong is most important in seeing value in life and in coping with intensely painful emotions."

— Karyn Hall, PhD

Appendix: Research Methodology

QUANTITATIVE RESEARCH

For the quantitative data in this report, we surveyed a nationally representative sample of one thousand 13-to-25-year-olds in the United States. The study was in the field from September to October 2019. The sample was weighted for age, sex, and region to match the demographics of the country and produces a margin of error of +/- 3%. The age, sex, and racial demographics of this sample are as follows:

Age	Valid Percent
13 to 17	38%
18 to 22	30%
23 to 25	32%
Total	**100%**

Sex	Valid Percent
Female	48.5%
Male	50.8%
Other	0.7%
Total	**100%**

Race	Valid Percent
White	64%
Hispanic or Latino	14%
Black or African American	11%
American Indian or Alaska Native	1%
Asian	7%
Native Hawaiian/Pacific Islander	0%
Other	2%

QUALITATIVE RESEARCH

For the qualitative research, we conducted 35 in-depth interviews, either in person or via telephone. Interviews focused on understanding the pathways that lead young people to groups where they experience belongingness. Conversations were guided but open-ended, allowing for as much direction as possible from the interviewee. Interviews were transcribed and then analyzed thematically.

Interviews and survey responses are confidential and all names in this report are pseudonyms unless otherwise indicated. For more information or to obtain the survey instrument or request access to data sets, please contact us at *research@springtideresearch.org*.

Acknowledgments

Research Team:

Josh Packard, PhD, Executive Director

Megan Bissell, MA, Research Director

Adrianna Smell, MA, Research Assistant

Horizon Worden, MA, Research Assistant

Writing Team:

Josh Packard, PhD

John M. Vitek, MA

Jerry Ruff, MA

Brian Singer-Towns, MThS

Ellen B. Koneck, MAR

Creative Design and Production Team:

Steven Mino

Sigrid Lindholm

Becky Gochanour

Printed in the United States of America

5928 (PO6523)

ISBN 978-1-64121-089-8

REFERENCES

Page 8—Cigna. "Cigna's U.S. Loneliness Index: Survey of 20,000 Americans Examining Behaviors Driving Loneliness in the United States." May 2018.

Page 9—Ford Motor Company. "Looking Further with Ford: 2020 Trends Report." December 2019.

Page 39—Gallup, Inc. Confidence in Institutions polling. 2019.

Page 60—J. T. Cacioppo, J. H. Fowler, and N. A. Christakis. "Alone in the Crowd: The Structure and Spread of Loneliness in a Large Social Network." *Journal of Personality and Social Psychology,* December 2009.

Page 66—YouTube video: "Charles Taylor and Jonathan Sacks on The Future of Religion." TVO Docs, February 10, 2012.

Page 72—Hall, Karyn. "Create a Sense of Belonging." *Pieces of Mind* (blog). *Psychology Today,* March 24, 2014.

PHOTO CREDITS

(All photos appear on Unsplash unless otherwise indicated.)

Pages 2–3—Michael Pfister

Page 6—Vaisakh Shabu

Page 9—Eliott Reyna

Page 11—Carles Rabada

Pages 12–13—Warren Wong

Page 14—Cassandra Hamer

Page 17—Shannon VanDenHeuvel

Page 20—Jenn Lopez

Pages 26–27—Zachary Staines

Page 28—Ezra Jeffrey-Comeau

Page 31—Jordan McDonald

Pages 34–35—Devin Avery

Page 36—Alexis Brown

Page 41—No-Te Eksarunchai (Shutterstock)

Page 44—Rachel (@noguidebook)

Page 47—Mikael Frivold

Page 48—digitalskillet (Shutterstock)

Page 50—Rainier Ridao

Page 52—Adam Wilson

Page 54–55—Jonathan Bean

Page 56—Hatham (@hatham)

Page 61—Warren Wong

Page 72—Michael Henry

Ready to go deeper into the Belongingness Process?

Visit Springtide's website for a variety of resources to help you cultivate a sense of belonging with the young people in your own community and context. For blog posts, podcast conversations, or to sign up for our newsletter, go to *springtideresearch.org*.

Join the conversation, and connect with us on social media. Follow @WeAreSpringtide on Facebook, Instagram, and Twitter.

Share how you're developing belonging relationships with the young people in your circle of care. Send us a note at *stories@springtideresearch.org*.